THE GOSPEL OF KING DAVID

Philip Holdway-Davis

THE GOSPEL OF KING DAVID

Publisher
Insurance Professional Limited

Copyright © 2021
Philip Holdway-Davis

PO Box 11-603
Ellerslie
Auckland 1542
New Zealand

www.thesoulsong.co.nz
Created by: Philip Holdway-Davis

Copyright quotation rights:
Commercial Use
You must receive permission from Philip Holdway-Davis

Private, Personal & Not-for-Profit Use
This book is free to use for personal and not-for-profit use. Also freely use it for reprinting, quoting and public speaking. The words "used with the permission of Philip Holdway-Davis www.thesoulsong.co.nz" must appear at the end of the quotation(s).

ISBN 978-0-473-53208-6 (Softcover)
ISBN 978-0-473-53209-3 (Epub)

Printed in New Zealand

Contents

Introduction 1

The Prayer of Jesus 3

The SoUL Song – Short Version 4

Introduction to: The Gospel of King David 6

THE GOSPEL OF KING DAVID 8

Holy Spirit Magic 14

The Good Confession 23

Introduction

This is the second book of written miracles that belongs to the collection of the four books of written miracles now known as *The Four Gospels-In-Advance*. *The Four Gospels-In-Advance* in turn belongs to the collection of thirty books known as the *Scriptures of Unconditional Love*. *The Gospel of King David* is another ancient prophecy and prediction book concerning the appearance of *The Christ*. This prophecy was made around one thousand years before Christ appeared. Just as with *The Gospel of Isaiah*, it was miraculously fulfilled with pin-point accuracy by Jesus of Bethlehem and Nazareth.

The written miracle prophecies and predictions of both *The Gospel of Isaiah* & *The Gospel of King David* belong alongside a large number of prophecies from the Holy Bible's Old Testament. There are so many of them that they could only have been put there by Holy Spirit. I urge you to read *The Gospel of Isaiah* to find out more about this. You will also find explanations on *The Prayer of Jesus* and *The SoUL Song*.

I repeat from *The Gospel of Isaiah*, that whilst this miracle Gospel is short in length, it is full of GOD's power and potency. These supernatural Words are worth more than pure gold. Everything of value according to this world will rot and disappear, but the Words in *The Gospel of Isaiah* will never pass away but will remain with us forever (Luke 21:33).

I have added a new component to be used with the worship components in *The Gospel of Isaiah: Healing & Working of Miracles*. I would like everyone to ask GOD for such gifts. Many of you reading or hearing *The Gospel of Isaiah* & *The Gospel of King David* will no longer be in two minds and question in your hearts whether these things are true or not. Instead, you will now know, beyond any reasonable or rational doubt, that these things are indeed true and that nothing really exists outside of the truth. All these truths are certain, powerful, and established on a sure footing. You will now have confidence to ask EHYER to give you these Holy Spirit gifts of GOD so that you can continue to do the work of Jesus by destroying the works of Devil-Satan. By healing and restoring people, animals, and everything organic, you will be glorifying the Name of GOD which is EHYER.

The Prayer of Jesus

Come near and draw close to GOD and GOD will draw near to you
– James 4:8

The Spirit of Jesus is EHYER ASHER EHYER which is the Name GOD told Moses when asked (Exodus 3:14).

Jesus told us to use these words when talking to GOD:

"Our Father in Heaven,
May your Name be kept Holy,
Your Kingdom come,
Your Will be done on earth as it is in heaven.
Give us enough bread to eat today.
Forgive us our sin as we have forgiven those who have sinned against us.
Do not allow us to be tempted but deliver us from the Evil One.
Yours is the power and the glory forever and ever."

- *The Witness of The Twelve Apostles.*

The SoUL Song

Short Version

EHYER ASHER EHYER
IHU KARAITI
EGO SUM QUI SUM
I AM WHO AM

EHYER ASHER EHYER
I AM THE WAY
I AM THE TRUTH
I AM THE LIFE

EHYER ASHER EHYER
I AM THE LIGHT
I AM THE DOOR
I AM THE GOOD

EHYER ASHER EHYER
I AM THE SHEPHERD
I AM THE BREAD
I AM THE VINE

EHYER ASHER EHYER
I AM THE RESURRECTION
I AM THE START
I AM THE END

EHYER ASHER EHYER
I AM THE ALPHA
I AM THE OMEGA
I AM WHO AM

EHYER ASHER EHYER
Baptise me with Your Spirit
In the Name of the Father
Son & Holy Spirit

EHYER ASHER EHYER
IHU KARAITI REPUTE
Heal my heart and spirit
Heal my body and mind

EHYER ASHER EHYER
IHU KARAITI
EGO SUM QUI SUM
I AM WHO AM

Introduction To:
The Gospel of King David

David, which means "the beloved" in Hebrew, was the youngest son of Jesse of Bethlehem, of the house of Judah, a descendant of Abraham, Isaac, Jacob, Rahab (ex-prostitute), Boaz and Ruth. He was also the ancestor of Joseph, husband of (virgin) Mary, and therefore the ancestor of Jesus as well. Bethlehem is the City of David, the same place where Jesus was born. A famous song was written about it called *Once in Royal David's City*:

Once in royal David's city,
Stood a lowly cattle shed,
Where a mother laid her baby
In a manger for His bed:
Mary was that mother mild,
Jesus Christ her little child.

David started well as the shepherd boy who killed the giant Goliath with a single stone in his slingshot. From there he went from strength to strength winning battles as GOD enabled him. He became the King of Israel as EHYER had said, *"Here is a man after my own heart."* Then, one day he stopped fighting and rested in his palace. He committed adultery with Bathsheba and murdered her husband.

Karma (GOD's Judgement) ensued quickly and it ended badly. We learn from this lesson to keep busy moving forward with the Will of EHYER instead of resting. If we choose to be lazy then disaster awaits us. It was instant karma for David as he was not allowed to build the temple and his son Absalom tried to overthrow him. Because of this, David became quite a sad old man. Nevertheless, the Holy Spirit was able to input inspiration into David to write some Psalms for us. Just consider Psalm 22; it's as though David is in the place of Jesus looking down upon the scene before him while being executed.

THE GOSPEL of KING DAVID

(Psalm 22)

Prophecy Made: 1,000 BC

Prediction Fulfilled: AD 33 by Jesus of Bethlehem and Nazareth

THE PROPHECY

My GOD, my GOD, why have You forsaken me? Why are You far away from saving me, from the words of my distress?

My GOD, I call you all day, but You do not answer – also by night, continually without stopping.

But You are holy, living in the praises of Israel.

Our Fathers trusted You. They trusted, and You always rescued them.

They cried to You and got away safely. They trusted You and were never put to shame.

But I am a worm and not a man. I am scorned by man and despised by people.

All who see me laugh at me. Insults stream out of their mouths. They shake their heads saying, "He committed himself to GOD, let GOD save him! Let GOD rescue him because GOD's pleased with him!"

For You are the person who brought me from the womb, the person who caused me to trust when suckling my mother's breasts.

I was thrown onto You from birth, You have been my GOD ever since I left my mother's womb.

Do not be too far from me because trouble is afoot and there is nobody else to help.

Many young bulls have surrounded me. Powerful bulls from Bashan have encircled me.

They have opened their mouths against me like vicious, roaring lions.

I have been poured out like water, and all my bones are dislocated. My heart is like wax. It has melted deep inside me.

My strength has dried up like a piece of broken pottery. My tongue sticks to my mouth. You have placed me in the dust of death.

Dogs have surrounded me. An evil mob has encircled me. They have pierced my hands and feet.

I can count all my bones. People stare and they gloat over me.

They divide my clothes among themselves. They cast lots for my clothing.

Do not be away, my GOD. You are my strength, hurry and help me.

Deliver my soul from the sword, my life from vicious dogs.

Save me from the lion's mouth and from the horns of wild bulls. You have answered me.

I will declare Your Name to my brothers. I will praise You in the middle of the congregation.

All who fear GOD, praise him! All you descendants of Jacob, glorify him! Stand in awe of him, all you descendants of Israel.

GOD has not despised or hated the affliction of the oppressed one. He has not hidden his face from him. GOD heard when the afflicted one cried out to him for help.

My praise comes from You while I am in the midst of the congregation. I will fulfil my solemn promises amongst those who reverently trust, and are in awe, of GOD.

Humble and gentle people will eat until they are full. Those who seek GOD will praise him. May your hearts live forever.

Throughout the whole earth, people will remember and return to GOD. All families from all nations will worship You.

The only rightful king is GOD and his dominion is the nations.

All prosperous people on earth will eat and will bow down. Before him all those who go down to the dust will kneel in front of him, including those who are only just alive.

There will be descendants who serve him, it will be declared to a generation the things of GOD.

They will tell people who have yet to be born about GOD's righteousness, that he has completed this.

PREDICTION FULFILMENT
(Matthew, Mark, Luke & John)

They took Jesus to a place known as Golgotha or "The Place of the Skull". They tried to offer him wine there, which was mixed with myrrh, but he did not drink it.

They crucified him.

After the soldiers had crucified Jesus, they divided up his garments into four portions, and each soldier had one. The tunic remained but it was seamless because it was made as a one-piece from top to bottom. The soldiers then discussed it and decided, *"We should not rip it. Let us cast lots for it instead, to see who wins it."* This fulfilled the Scripture:

"They divided my garments up between them, then cast lots for my clothing."

Therefore, that is what the soldiers actually did.

People that passed by poured abuse on him, shaking their heads saying, *"You said you were going to destroy the temple and rebuild it in three days, now go and save yourself! If you really are the Son of GOD, get yourself down from the execution wood! He's supposed to trust in GOD so let's see if GOD saves him, that is, if GOD wants him. After all, he did say, 'I am the Son of GOD.'"*

In exactly the same manner, the religious rulers and scribes laughed at him between themselves, saying, *"He so-called 'saved' others, yet he can't even save himself! Now, let's see the Messiah, the King of Israel himself, get off this execution wood. If he does that, then we will believe him."* Those who were crucified with him also criticised and taunted him.

From between twelve noon until three in the afternoon, the land was smothered in darkness. At 3.00 pm, Jesus shouted out loudly, *"Eloi, Eloi, lema sabachthani?"* which means, *"My GOD, My GOD, why have You forsaken me?"*

Having said this, knowing that everything had now been successfully accomplished, and also to fulfil the Scriptures, Jesus said, *"I thirst."* Some sour wine was sitting there in a jar. So, they soaked a sponge in the wine, placed it onto a twig of hyssop, and raised it up for him to drink of it. Upon Jesus receiving the sour wine, he exclaimed, *"It is finished!"* Then bowing his head, he gave up his spirit.

Now it was the *Day of Preparation*, and the next day was a *High Sabbath*. So that the dead bodies would not be on the execution wood whilst the Sabbath was on, the Jews asked Pilate to break their legs and have their bodies taken away. Therefore, the soldiers arrived and broke the legs of the first man who had been crucified with Jesus along with those of the other.

However, when they came to Jesus, they realised that he was already dead, therefore, they did not break his legs. To make sure, a soldier pierced his side with a spear. Immediately, blood and water flowed out from the piercing.

All these things happened for the Scripture to be fulfilled: *"None of his bones will be broken."* Also, according to another Scripture: *"They will look on the One who they have pierced."* (Zechariah 12:10)

"Look, he is coming amongst the clouds, and every eye will look at him – including those who pierced him. All the peoples throughout the earth will weep because of him. It will be! Amen"
...When I looked at him, I fell down at his feet as if I had just died. Yet he put his right hand on me and said, "Don't be scared. I am the Beginning and the End, the Living One. I was dead, and look, now I am alive forever and ever! Now I hold the keys of Death and of Hell." (Revelation 1:7 & 17-18)

HOLY SPIRIT MAGIC

My friend Ray in New Zealand, in the '90s, had a bad back. He was in a lot of pain and sometimes found it difficult to go to work or even get up from bed. The medical doctors and specialists were unable to help so he went to his church elders and they prayed for him and anointed him with oil (James 5:14). There was no change in his condition. Then, against the advice of some from his church, he went to a Maori healer. The Maori healer touched his back, said that he had found "it", and then healed "it". Maori are a highly spiritual people.

This is rather like the event dealt with below where an old woman, as a last resort, came to Jesus for healing. Ray's back was healed in accordance with James 5:14, but he first had to continue asking (just like the other woman in the event shown below) and not give up. There were those in the church that opposed him seeing a Maori healer, but as it turned out, the Maori healer had the faith and Jesus chose to heal, at that time, through the Maori healer and not through the church elders. GOD had given this Maori person a gift of healing.

Having stated the above, a Lloyds underwriter I knew in the late '70s called Len, had damaged his back in a British Army Land Rover accident. He had to regularly get up from his seat at his box in Lloyds of London to walk around for relief from the pain. When I returned to Lloyds after a three-year stint in the army in Northern Ireland, Len had been healed. A person from a Christian church had the "gift of healing" and Jesus had healed Len through him.

I would like as many people as possible to receive the Holy Spirit gifts of healing and working of miracles. Actually, I would like you, the reader or hearer, to receive them. By doing so, you can follow the example of Jesus and go around destroying the works of Devil-Satan.

DESTROYING THE DEVIL'S WORKS

The reason the Son of GOD came to earth was with the ultimate aim of destroying the Devil's works – 1 John 3:8

John said, *"Rabbi, we came across a man driving out demons in your Name, so we told him to stop it because he was not part of our group". Jesus replied, "You should not stop him, because nobody who does a miracle in my Name will be able to say anything bad about me afterwards. Whoever is not against us is for us."* – Mark 9: 38-39

The *Scriptures of Unconditional Love* tell us that we are observing the phasing-out of death. In the above verse, a miracle is performed by a man not aligned to any official group. This means that you and I are free to continue working with Christ as individuals to destroy Devil-Satan's work. We do not need to have any alignment with, or permission from, any group or person – whether a church, mosque, temple, religious organisation, or any of their leaders.

Everything organic can be helped, saved, or healed in the Name of Jesus. It was all originally part of GOD anyway but without the death in it. Calling on the Name of EHYER brings life and destroys death. So, go ahead and use Holy Spirit magic to apply Holy Spirit material (material with no death in it i.e. GOD's Name, Spirit, Unconditional Love & Word applied in this material world of Maya) to everything that is organic – people, animals, plants and everything in all creation. We are told to declare this Good News Gospel to all creation – Mark 16:15.

Speak Holy Spirit Words, which is EHYER, over everything that is needy. Touch creation with your hands or touch the recipient with the books of *Scriptures of Unconditional Love* as they contain a lot of Holy Spirit material – especially *The Gospel of Isaiah, The Gospel of King David, The Gospel of Moses, The Gospel of The Prophets (The Four Gospels-In-Advance)* and the *Witness of Jesus*. Holy Spirit material is the physical substance of GOD, which is Word, Spirit, Unconditional Love & Name. By reciting or singing or hearing GOD's Name (such as in The SoUL Song) you are applying Holy Spirit material to the person, animal, creature, or plant.

Young or old, male, or female, black or white, able, or unable, everybody can apply Holy Spirit substance to anything that is not well. This is Holy Spirit magic. It needs to be done consistently and without any doubt or negative words. I hope everyone will become skilled in using Holy Spirit magic. Jesus had his own power but there are a number of lessons he showed us for our use. Here are a few of them:

The Woman and the Judge – Luke 18:1-8

Then Jesus told his disciples a parable to impress upon them that they should always pray and not lose heart. *"In a certain town there was a judge who neither feared GOD nor cared for other people. There was a widow in that town who kept coming to him saying, 'Give me justice against the person opposing me.'*

"For a long time he refused, but in the end he reasoned to himself, 'I don't fear GOD and have no respect for other people, but because this woman keeps pestering me, I will see that she gets her justice – otherwise she'll wear me out pestering me!'"

Then the LORD explained, *"Observe what the unjust judge said. Will GOD not bring about justice for his chosen people, who cry out to him day and night? Will he keep delaying them? I tell you; he will quickly judge in their favour. But, when the Son of Man comes, will he find such trust on earth?"*

Lesson: Never stop pestering GOD.

Jairus's Daughter – Mark 5:21-43

Jesus crossed to the other side of the lake by boat and a sizeable crowd gathered around him. One of the synagogue officials, called Jairus, approached him and fell at his feet. He pleaded desperately with him, *"My little daughter is near death, please come and lay your hands on her so that she will get well and live."*

Jesus went with him. A large crowd followed pressing all around him. A woman was there who had haemorrhaged for twelve years.

She had suffered much under many physicians and had spent all her money, but instead of getting better she got worse. She heard about Jesus so came up behind him in the crowd and touched his robe. She thought, *"Even if I just touch his clothing, I will be healed."* Instantly her bleeding stopped, and she felt in her body that she had been healed of her disease.

Immediately Jesus knew that power had gone out of him. He turned around in the crowd and asked, *"Who touched my clothing?"*

"You see the people pressing up against you and yet you ask who touched you?" his disciples said.

But Jesus kept looking around to see who had done it. The woman, frightened and fearful because she knew what had happened to her, came forward and fell at his feet and told him the whole truth. Jesus said to her, *"Daughter, your trust has healed you. Go in peace and be healed from your disease."*

While still speaking, people came from Jairus's house and said, *"Your daughter is dead, don't bother the teacher anymore."*

Jesus ignored them and told the synagogue official, *"Don't be afraid; just trust me."*

Nobody was allowed to follow him except Peter, James, and John the brother of James. When they came to the synagogue official's house there was a commotion, people were crying and wailing loudly. Jesus went in and said to them, *"Why all this commotion and crying? The child hasn't died, she's merely asleep."* They ridiculed him.

Jesus had them all chucked out. Then he took the child's father and mother and those disciples with him and went to see the child.

He took her hand and said to her, *"Talitha kumi!"* (Little girl, I tell you to get up!"). Instantly the girl got up and started walking around – she was twelve years old. Everyone was completely amazed. Jesus gave strict orders not to tell anybody about what had just happened, then he told them to feed the child.

Lesson: It is OK to come to Jesus for salvation or healing after all other options have failed. Whatever Jesus says will eventually happen. Don't listen to doubters and don't join their negativity; keep your mouth firmly shut! Say nothing and let GOD's Word happen. It would have been tempting for Jairus to blame his daughter's death on Jesus being held up by the woman. Instead, he believed Jesus and not the negative doubters. Mark 4:35-41 is another example where Jesus's words *"let's cross to the other side"* **proved true when his disciples doubted in the face of a windstorm disaster. Both Jairus and the sick woman humbled themselves. Our attitude should also be one of humility before GOD.**

"...so is my word that goes out from my mouth – It will not return to me unfulfilled, but will accomplish what I want and achieve the successful result for which I sent it." Isaiah 55:11

Healing Disciples – Matthew 10:1 & 7-8

Jesus called together his twelve disciples to him and gave them authority to drive out unclean spirits and to heal every kind of disease and weakness... *"As you go, proclaim 'the kingdom of heaven is close by'. Heal the sick, raise the dead, cleanse those who have* leprosy, drive out demons. Freely you have received, so freely give without asking for payment."

Lesson: Jesus has never cancelled, withdrawn or changed those instructions. This means you can consider yourself commissioned by Jesus to go and do likewise. Know this for certain: GOD's Word will never return empty or unfulfilled. – Isaiah 55:11

King Hezekiah Granted Extra Fifteen Years of Life – Isaiah 38:1-5

In those days, Hezekiah became ill to the point of death. Isaiah the prophet, son of Amoz, went to him and said, *"Here is what GOD says: 'Put your house in order, because you are going to die; you will not survive.'"*

Hezekiah turned his face to the wall and prayed to GOD, *"I implore you, GOD, to remember that I have lived before you truthfully and with my heart's devotion. I have done what is good in your eyes."* Then Hezekiah cried bitterly.

Then the word of GOD came to Isaiah: *"Go and tell Hezekiah, 'this is what the GOD of your ancestor David, says: 'I have heard your prayer and seen your tears; because of that I will now add an extra fifteen years to your life.'"*

Lesson: Turning to GOD alone and asking GOD for something with true tears can change GOD's decision on anything, even a death.

Your Holy Spirit Gift – 1 Corinthians 12:7-11

"Now to each individual person is given a particular showing of the Spirit than can be used for the common good. To each person through the Spirit is given:
- Wisdom
- Word of knowledge
- Faith
- Gifts of healing
- Working of miracles
- Prophecy
- Ability to judge between spirits
- Speaking in different kinds of tongues
- Interpretation of tongues.

All these are the work of one and the same Spirit, and he distributes them to each one, just as he chooses." – The Apostle Paul.

Lesson: When you engage with GOD eagerly ask for the Holy Spirit gift of healing and miracle-working because, in verse 31, we are told to eagerly desire the greater gifts. Be content with whatever gift the Holy Spirit gives you. Never lose sight of the fact that the whole of the next chapter in 1 Corinthians 13 is dedicated to Unconditional Love which is greater than any gift of the Holy Spirit.

Spread the word around to everyone that they should go and get a Holy Spirit gift and apply Holy Spirit magic against Devil-Satan. In Matthew 5:45 Jesus said, *"...that you may be children of your Father in heaven. He causes his sun to rise on the evil and the good, and sends rain on the righteous and the unrighteous."* This means that everyone, excluding no-one, is eligible to receive a Holy Spirit gift – even the sinful! So, don't say "I am not worthy", "I am a sinner", "I am too bad". Rubbish! Christ took the punishment for all of our sins in our place. It's done, it's over. You are now set free to serve GOD with immediate effect!

The Good Confession

We agree with the apostles and believe that there is only one Healer who is made of both flesh and spirit, born and unborn, GOD in the flesh, true life surrounded by death, son of Mary and Son of GOD, initially experiencing suffering then afterwards beyond suffering – Jesus the Christ, our RULER.

For our GOD, Jesus the Christ:

- ♥ Was conceived in Mary's womb according to the pre-planning of GOD and by the Holy Spirit

- ♥ Is physically descended from the line of David according to ancestry

- ♥ Is the Son of GOD according to the will and power of GOD

- ♥ Was born the son of Mary when she was still a virgin

- ♥ Ate and drank among us, both before being killed and after being raised up to life again

- ♥ Was baptised by John in order that all righteousness might be fulfilled by him

- ♥ Was nailed and crucified for us in his physical body under Pontius Pilate and Herod the Tetrarch

- ♥ Died in full sight of persons in heaven, on earth, and under the earth

- ♥ Was physically and spiritually raised from the dead when his Father raised him up

- ♥ Was touched and handled by his disciples after his resurrection. His disciples then saw that he was composed of flesh whilst being spiritually united with the Father at the same time. For this reason, his disciples also treated death with the same contempt.

He suffered all these things for our sakes so that we might be saved and likewise be raised up from the dead by the Father if we exercise trust in Jesus the Christ.

He has raised up a standard for all ages through his resurrection, to rally together his holy and faithful people whether among Jews or non-Jews, in the one body of the community of GOD's people.

Other Books by Philip Holdway-Davis:

Triumph on the Western Front

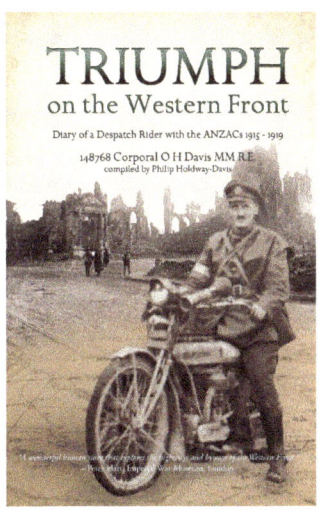

ISBN: 9-780473-314637

Share the experiences of a Despatch Rider during World War I by reading his own words written as a diary during his years on the Western Front. As an author of a dozen books, a journalist and a decent Christian Church of England man, Oswald writes descriptively and takes you on a journey through his eyes during WWI. He puts you on his trusty steed, his 1915 Triumph motorcycle, and dashes you around the battlefields of the Somme and Ypres.

Oswald Harcourt Davis joined the Royal Engineers in 1916 and arrived in Abbeville, Somme, France in July that year. He was attached to the ANZACs and dished out a Triumph motorcycle to carry pigeons and vital messages at a time when communications were limited and risky.

Read in fascinating detail his journeys around the Somme and Ypres Salient areas and the difficulties he had to face. Ever facing the danger of being "bumped" and "knocked" he rose to duty's call and made sure the pigeons got through. He cheated death on several occasions and admits he was scared and on the brink of cowardice, yet he was brave enough for decoration. He was awarded the Military Medal at Messines.

The book is available for free download or purchase by inserting the following address into your browser: www.triumphonthewesternfront.com.

ISBN: 978-0-473-53206-2

THE GOSPEL OF ISAIAH

The Gospel of Isaiah is the first of *The Four Gospels-In-Advance* collection of written miracles. There is no other explanation. It was written about 600 years before the time of Jesus of Bethlehem and Nazareth and fulfilled accurately by Ihu Te Karaiti (Jesus the Christ) sometime around AD 33-36. This book focuses mainly on Isaiah chapter 53 – "The Banned Chapter". Most (if not all) Jewish synagogues around the world refuse to read it because they claim it causes arguments and confusion. The actual truth is that Isaiah 53 is a compelling witness that Jesus of Bethlehem and Nazareth really was, and is, the Christ-Messiah. Synagogues do not want to admit this and are still waiting for the Christ-Messiah to come. At some stage in the future, the Jews will recognise Jesus as their Messiah when the full number of non-Jews has come into the Kingdom of Jesus (Romans 11:24-26). Make up your own mind by reading this book and all the supernatural prophecies contained in it.

The Gospel of Isaiah is FREE to download or purchase at www.thesoulsong.co.nz

www.ingramcontent.com/pod-product-compliance
Lightning Source LLC
Chambersburg PA
CBHW062029290426
44108CB00025B/2834